WINTER

DISCOVERING THE SEASONS

Written by Louis Santrey

Photography by Francene Sabin

Troll Associates

Library of Congress Cataloging in Publication Data

Santrey, Louis.
   Winter.

   (Discovering the seasons)
   Summary: Describes the changes that take place in the
natural world during the period of the year when days
are shortest and temperatures lowest.
      1. Winter—Juvenile literature.   2. Seasons—
Juvenile literature.   [1. Winter.   2. Seasons]
I. Sabin, Francene, ill.   II. Title.   III. Series:
Santrey, Louis. Discovering the seasons.
QB631.S26   1983   508   82-19353
ISBN 0-89375-907-4 (case)
ISBN 0-89375-908-2 (pbk.)

Cover photo by Colour Library International.

*For their special photo contributions, the publisher
wishes to thank: Janice Lozano, pages 4, 24 (bottom),
26 (left), 30; Melody Norsgaard-Ashe, pages 9 (right),
14 (left), 24 (top); L & M Photography/FPG, page 21
(left).*

10   9   8   7   6   5   4   3   2   1

The bright reds and golds of autumn are gone. All the leaves have fallen, and the trees stand bare against the sky. Chill winds rattle the leafless branches like the bones of a skeleton. Each day is colder than the one before as winter marches closer and closer.

Every day the sun rises a minute or two later in the morning, and sets a minute or two earlier in the afternoon. As the December days grow shorter, the dark winter nights grow longer. The sun's rays are weak and pale. They can no longer warm the woods and the lake. In December comes the shortest day of the year—it is the first day of winter.

In the summer, the woods were filled with birds. They built their nests in tall trees, safely hidden by a thick cover of leaves. Now that the trees are bare, the nests can be seen. But most of the birds are gone. They have flown far to the South, where the weather is warm.

In the summer, the woods were also filled with insects. But, like the birds, they are gone now. Some insects have flown away to warm places. Some are asleep in their winter homes under the ground. And some laid thousands of eggs on the branches of trees and bushes, while the weather was still warm. Then these insects died, leaving their eggs to hatch in the spring.

Wasp eggs spend the winter in hard, brown shells. Each shell looks like a round nut clinging to the branch of a tree. The gypsy moth lays a mass of eggs in a sticky, yellow patch on tree trunks and branches. Other insects lay their eggs on leaves and twigs, on the ground, and in dead logs.

Some animals are sleeping away the cold winter months, but not all of them. The timid deer comes out of the woods to search for food. It finds carrots in a nearby farmyard, then quickly darts back into the safety of the woods. The frisky squirrel is busy all winter, eating acorns, other nuts, and seeds.

During the cold, bitter winter, the ground is frozen
hard. After it rains, the water cannot seep into the
soil. It lies on top of the hard ground, then freezes
into pools of ice that trap living trees and dead
wood. The vine of a wild grape plant becomes a
curved icicle, glittering in the sunlight.

There is a rare beauty to the cold season. Strange and wonderful forms are shaped by the wind and frost. A shape that looks like a face is carved in the ice. The spiky fruit of the sweet gum tree sits on a sheet of ice that is dotted with tiny air bubbles. A dead oak leaf is trapped within.

One day the sky grows dark. Fat snowflakes float down, down, down. A soft, white blanket is spread over the field and forest floor. When the sun breaks through the clouds, the snow glistens. Here and there, green shoots of grass bravely poke through the mounds of snow.

Most plants have lost their colors, but not all. The sturdy holly, with its tough, shiny, green leaves, stands erect in the snow. The hawthorn berries are bright red. They probably will not last the winter. Before spring comes, they will be eaten by cottontail rabbits, bobwhites, foxes, and pheasants.

Even in the middle of the day the winter sun does not rise high in the sky. It cannot warm the world below. The snow will not melt on the forest floor. It is a coat of white that will remain until the warmth of spring thaws it.

A rotting tree stump looks lifeless in the forest. But deep inside the soft wood, tiny things are alive or waiting to be born. The stump is a warm, dry home, where insect eggs safely spend the long weeks of winter. The white termite is one of the creatures that makes its home in decaying wood.

The pondweeds are locked into the ice. Their tops are dry and brown. Nothing moves on the surface of the water except the wind. But below, out of sight, there is life. Fish swim around slowly. Newts, salamanders, slugs, and snails are burrowed deep in the muddy bottom of the pond. They will wait out the winter there.

Most of the birds have flown south for the winter, but many have stayed behind. There is the tiny nuthatch. This is the only bird that can hop down a tree head first. The gray tufted titmouse sings *peter-peter-peter* as it clings to a branch.

The noisy blue jay is busy all winter chasing away cats, squirrels, and smaller birds. Two finches perch together in a tree. All these winter birds spend long hours each day in search of food. There are no worms to pull from the ground, no insects flying through the air, no soft green grasses. The birds must hunt for seeds, acorns, and berries.

One dark night, snow begins to fall. It does not stop until the next evening. The snow is very deep. Everything looks ghostly for miles and miles. Then the wind, like an artist, carves the snow into fantastic shapes that look like ocean waves, sand dunes, and mountains on the moon.

It is so cold that the whole world seems to have frozen solid. A snowy cliff is turned into a wall of thick, blue-white ice. There was a time, millions of years ago, when much of North America was covered with ice like this!

Wild ducks sit on the ice of a frozen pond. All morning they have been feeding on acorns in the nearby woods. It is a bone-chilling afternoon, but the ducks are not cold. Under their smooth, glossy feathers is a thick layer of fat. This keeps them warm in the coldest weather.

Ice crystals are among Nature's most beautiful creations. They look like needles, stars, strands of silvery tinsel. New crystal shapes are formed every time the temperature changes a few degrees. But it must stay below freezing—32 degrees Fahrenheit, or zero degrees Celsius—or they will melt.

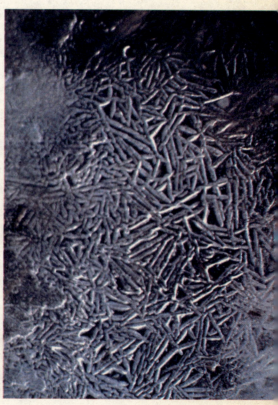

Many woodland animals stay hidden in their nests and burrows during winter days. They do this for safety. They know their enemies can spot them very easily against the white snow. That is why these animals come out only at night, when they have the cover of darkness.

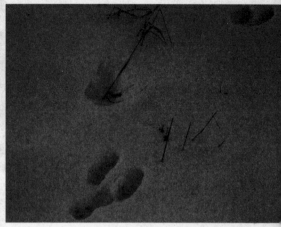

In the silent, early-morning hours, there are signs of activity on the snowy forest floor. The white carpet is marked by the tracks of animals that roam at night. The tracks show that deer, rabbits, foxes, field mice, and other woodland creatures have passed this way.

The need for food forces the animals out of their warm homes to face the deep freeze of February. But it is very hard to find things to eat. There are no piles of acorns under the oak tree and no soft leaves and buds. The squirrel scurries about, trying to find some of the acorns it buried last autumn. The lynx uses its large feet like snowshoes to move quickly across the snow in search of prey.

There are signs that the animals have not been starving. Strips of bark have been pulled from a birch tree by deer. The twigs of a young tree have been chewed by rabbits. And bittersweet berries have been taken from a vine by birds.

The distant mountain peaks are still capped with snow. But the days are growing longer, and the sun is getting warmer every day. At the pond the snow is beginning to melt. It brings the first promise of spring.

The nights are still freezing, but not the days. They no longer have the sting of winter. The wall of ice is losing its war with the warming rays of the sun. Melting ice turns to water and trickles down the rocks, feeding brooks and streams and rivers.

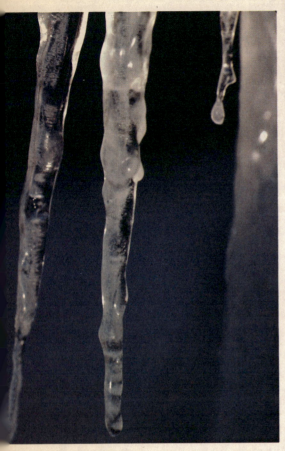

Every day, a little more ice and snow melt away.
But every night, winter again tightens its grip,
holding on as long as it can. With this continual
melting and freezing, Nature shapes and reshapes a
magic world of incredible ice forms.

Overnight the water freezes, etching curved lines at the edge of the lake. Pure white diamonds glitter on brittle branches. Crystal daggers dangle from a tree limb. Silvery caterpillars crawl from branch to branch. It is a brilliant show until the sun warms the ice back to water—and the frosty forms are gone.

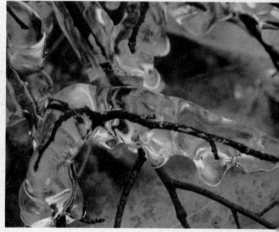

The last patches of snow cling to the side of a cliff like a frozen waterfall. The winds of early March whirl through the trees, singing the end of winter. The ground is softer, the sky is bluer, the air is fresh and sweet.

Nature's clock is ticking toward spring. Under the soft, brown soil, baby plants come to life. Bit by bit, they push upward, reaching for sunlight. One day nothing is there. The next day the tiniest shoots are peeping through the ground—the green leaves of the crocus and the reddish-brown tips of the lily of the valley.

One morning, delicate white blossoms open in the golden sunlight. These are the hardy little snow-drops, one of the first flowers to bloom every year. They are Nature's signal that another beautiful but frozen winter is over at last.